Dropshipping

*How to Create Passive Income with Online
Dropshipping!
A Step-by-Step Guide to Creating
Financial Freedom!*

Table of Contents

Chapter I:

What is Dropshipping and How Does it Work?

Drop shipping has become a very popular online business. But many people do not know what it actually means. Some of them even find it a bit intimidating to take up such a venture. This guide can be very useful for newcomers who wish to join the e-commerce world and earn up to $10k a month. Those who are interested in creating a passive income and aspire for financial freedom can easily bank on this book for step-by-step guidance.

After reading this handbook, you will understand the correct meaning of the term "dropshipping", and comprehend the way in which this business model functions. Moreover, it will be possible for you to assess if this type of enterprise is your cup of tea or not. If you seem to be made for it, then you will know how you should find the correct supplier and product to become an accomplished entrepreneur.

So, here's how to get ready for a flourishing e-commerce business!

Introduction

Dropshipping refers to a kind of business in which there is no need to maintain an inventory, own a warehouse and store the goods, or even ship the products to the customers on your own.

It is one of the various e-commerce models that can be found online. The word dropshipping became popular when Chinese e-commerce stores were launched in the US in 2006, and AliExpress gained popularity. Some smart entrepreneurs took advantage of it and set up their own stores to earn profits. They utilized AliExpress as its costs were low. Soon, more and more people started doing the same, and dropshipping became all the rage.

Nowadays, it is considered to be a very lucrative business model which can be set up with nearly zero investment. Zappos, Fab & Gilt, and Wayfair are some remarkable examples of businesses built around the dropshipping model.

Dropshipping is commonly used by the new entrepreneurs, mostly the Millennials and Gen Zers.

Delegating the shipping work to another person reduces the operational costs for the retailer and gives them more time to concentrate on making efforts for customer acquisition.

Dropshipping is a Business Model

It is a business model based on the management of the supply chain. In this, the retailers do not have to own an inventory. They promote the goods of suppliers. In turn, they earn a handsome commission.

Dropshippers act as intermediaries between the customers and the suppliers. They pass on the orders for goods to suppliers and keep a particular amount with themselves as commission. Then the suppliers dispatch the goods from the warehouse to their respective customers.

In this business model, the dropshipper sells the products for higher prices and earns a profit. For example, if the wholesale price of a product is $150, he may sell it at a price of $200 or $250 and thereby earn a commission equal to $50 and $100 respectively. In dropshipping, products are arbitraged for profits.

Private label dropshipping is one of the emerging trends in this type of business. In this, the manufacturer produces some custom item on the request of the retailer and dropships it. Such items include simple keepsakes, pictures, apparel which have custom logos, customized nutritional supplements and vitamins.

Main Features

The main features of dropshipping are:

- The dropshipper sets his own prices.

- It is possible to start wholesaling products without entering into a partnership with a manufacturer. Instead of this, he can use AliExpress, Amazon, or eBay for this purpose.

- Gaining profits through arbitrage.

The Way in which Dropshipping Works

In a dropshipping business, the retailer enters into a partnership with a supplier who manufactures, warehouses, packages, and ships the products to the customer on behalf of the retailer.

The procedure is as follows:

First, the customer visits the online store of the retailer and orders an item.

Next, the retailer manually or automatically forwards the details of the customer and the order placed by him, to his dropshipping supplier.

Finally, the supplier packs the items and ships them to the buyer directly in the name of the retailer.

An Illustration of the Dropshipping Process

A is an online retailer who sells customized T-shirts. He dropships all his goods directly from B who is a wholesaler. The customer C places an order with A.

Step 1: A Customer Places an Order

C wants to buy a customized T-shirt and orders for it through A's online store. After his order gets an approval, these things will take place:

- A and C will receive a confirmation of the order by email. This is mostly generated automatically by the software that is used in the store.

- The details of payment by C are noted, and the money is automatically deposited in A's bank account.

Step 2: The Retailer Places an Order with the Supplier

A will forward the order confirmation email to one sales representative of B. B will deduct the wholesale cost of the items and the processing and shipping charges from A's credit card.

Note: Some dropshippers support automatic uploading of orders or provide the facility to order online manually. But mostly email is used for placing an order with a dropshipping supplier.

Step 3: The Wholesaler Ships the Product

Assuming that the product is available in stock and B could successfully deduct the money from A's card, B will pack the T-shirt and send it to C directly.

Although B will send the item, A's name and his address will be on the label, and his logo will be there on the packing slip and invoice. After the shipment is finalized, B will send an invoice along with the tracking number through email to A.

Note: These orders are shipped very quickly, and the goods are delivered within a few hours. So, it is possible for the retailers to advertise that the orders will be delivered on the same day.

Step 4: The Retailer Alerts his Customer About the Shipment

After A receives a tracking number, he will send all the tracking details to C. He may send it through the built-in email interface of the store.

Once the order is shipped, payment is collected, and C is notified, the procedure for ordering and fulfilling the order is complete. A's profit is equal to the difference of the amount he charged from C and the amount he paid to B.

Note:

- The suppliers are not visible to the customers: Even though the suppliers play a vital role in this business model, they are not visible to the customer. The package received by the customer shows only the retailer's logo and address. If the customer receives a wrong package, he has to contact the retailer who will coordinate things at the back with the dropshipper and ask him to send the right thing.

- Retailers do not handle the products: In dropshipping the retailer's purchase products from third parties. The goods are shipped by those parties to the buyers directly. So, the retailers do not see or handle the products.

The Difference Between Dropshipping Manufacturers, Wholesalers, and Aggregators

Many times, people use these terms interchangeably

in e-commerce parlance. But they definitely do not mean the same thing.

- Manufacturer: The company that produces the goods on their own. They may have a dropshipping facility or not. If they provide a facility, it will be very helpful for the retailer—reducing extra expenditure on the middleman. It will be possible to operate at the most reasonable cost which in turn will improve the profit margins.

- Wholesaler: First he purchases a single kind of product in bulk from a manufacturer. Then he helps in packaging and shipping it to the buyers online by means of the retailer's e-commerce enterprises.

- Aggregator: The person who purchases different goods from various manufacturers and provides them to the retailer so that he can sell an assortment of things.

  Utilizing the services of an aggregator can help to solve a number of issues associated with dropshipping. They are:

1. There will be no need for paying shipping costs to multiple wholesalers.

2. It will take less time to send different orders to various vendors. This will prevent confusion, and the orders will be fulfilled without delay.

But the aggregators charge more money, and this can influence the profit margins.

Dropshipping refers to a service and not to a role

A retailer, manufacturer, or wholesaler, any of them can work as one dropshipper. In case, a manufacturer agrees to ship his products to your customers on your behalf it is considered to be dropshipping. In the same way, a retailer can also opt to dropship, but his prices will not be very competitive like the wholesaler's because he will not buy things directly from a manufacturer.

If you buy things from a dropshipper, it does not imply that you will get things at the wholesale prices.

Chapter II:
Why Invest in Dropshipping?
How is it Beneficial?

Although dropshipping profit margins generally range between 15% and 45%, luxury items and consumer durables like electronics and jewelry may yield 100% profit margins. It all depends on selecting the correct niche and finding the correct supplier for it and making an entry into a market which is not saturated with it already.

Using a manufacturer to supply the goods directly rather than a supplier or vendor can cut out the role of a middleman and thereby ensure higher profit margins.

Once the enterprise gains momentum and establishes itself, it can almost become a money minting machine which does not require much input. The dropshipping business owned by Irwin Dominguez is an outstanding example of an e-commerce enterprise which earned one million US dollars in a very short span of 8 months. It gives an idea of the latent potential of this business.

Is Dropshipping For You?

Dropshipping is a fantastic option for new arrivals in the world of e-commerce. It requires a low-investment and involves less risk. These features can be enchanting and enthralling for the first-timers who are just stepping into the field of online business.

This type of enterprise demands a very small size of capital, so it is an ideal choice for those who already own a store and an inventory as well. They can try out certain goods in the markets and find out how they perform before getting a big stock of those goods.

The people who aspire to get impressive profits right away may not find this model very satisfactory. In case, your main goal is to earn a profit then it is better to associate with the manufacturers directly. But the catch is that the manufacturers do not always provide the facility for dropshipping.

The profit margins in this type of business are relatively lower than the other models of business, like wholesaling and manufacturing. In dropshipping a brand which is a fresh startup may not do well because the final control over customer satisfaction by means of brand experience and branding does not rest with the retailer.

Some facts and figures that show dropshipping is a feasible business model.

- 22% to 33% of retailers who work online have adopted the dropshipping business model.

- In 2011, 34% of the goods that were sold through Amazon were dropshipped. That means products worth more than $14 billion were dropshipped from a single online marketplace.

- Average profits of manufacturers who dropship their products are calculated to be 18.33% more than that of manufacturers who use the traditional retail business models.

- E-commerce sales on a global level were more than $2 trillion. It is anticipated that it will increase further and become nearly four and a half trillion dollars by 2021.

Google Trends also shows that in the last few years there has been a massive rise in the number of people who are interested in the dropshipping business.

The Entrepreneurs for whom Dropshipping is Suitable

New Entrepreneur

Dropshipping is a chosen model for the people who are just taking the initial steps to sell things online. Basically, selling things online is not a cake walk. It takes time for an average marketer to learn and acquire a knack of driving traffic to his website and things like conversion optimization. This model gives them an inexpensive way to learn all this before making huge investments in the business.

Validating Entrepreneur

The dropshipping model is an amazing way to try out new products and startups. This type of business is perfect for entrepreneurs who need product validation prior to making any investments.

Walmart Entrepreneur

Dropshipping happens to be an ideal enterprise for people who wish to put up a wide assortment of items for sale. In a traditional form of business, it is not possible to sell many different items without spending a huge amount in acquiring an inventory. While this model can be used most suitable for this purpose without purchasing anything upfront.

Budget Entrepreneur

This kind of enterprise involves the least expenditure for selling things online as there is no necessity for purchasing an inventory. Therefore, it is a number one business model for entrepreneurs with a small budget or those who prefer to maintain the startup costs at a minimum level.

The Entrepreneurs for whom the Dropshipping Model is not Appropriate

Brand Oriented Entrepreneur

No doubt, establishing a long-lasting brand is a difficult task, but it is very rewarding. In the dropshipping business, it is even tougher to accomplish this task. The reason is that as a retailer you do not have much control over the factors which influence the customer experience.

For instance, there may be times when your customer purchases a product from which is already sold out by your supplier. You may feel uncomfortable and frustrated in such situations and find it difficult to coordinate the transactions between your supplier and the customer. This may prove to be a very unpleasant experience for the client.

Another way in which you do not hold the reins of your customer's experience is related to packaging. As the delivery part depends on the supplier, he may not put in much effort to please the customer with impressive packaging. Most of the time the items will be received by the customer in some ordinary brown box which is not a very attractive offer.

Moreover, as you do not ship the items yourself if a customer does not get the parcel you have to call the shipping company and settle matters. This may take a long time because you will have to deal with some busy representative of the company. Thus, you may not be able to satisfy the customer and get a good reputation.

An Entrepreneur Who Focuses on Margins

Most probably the most prominent issue associated with dropshipping is that there are very thin margins. Usually, the gross margins, that means the difference between the price at which you sell an item and the money you pay to the drop shipper, for traditional dropshipping goods are between 10% to 20%.

Advantages of Dropshipping

There are several aspects of this type of enterprise which are very advantageous. They are:

1. It can be set up very easily: You do not have to waste time and energy on assembling things and setting up the business. Just a few basic steps have to be taken to become a full-fledged trader. Put your best foot forward and choose a product, find a supplier, create a website for yourself, and sell your goods, that's it! Even a novice who is unfamiliar with the e-commerce enterprises can understand and follow these steps quite easily.

2. The amount of money required for setting up an online business is negligible: The traditional models of business involve a lot of investment to set up and perform the retail functions, for example, purchasing a space and inventory. This step is not necessary for dropshipping. So, the entire cost of setting up a physical business entity is eliminated. At most, you may

have to invest money for running the website which includes the cost of hosting, apps, theme and other things.

3. No need to be concerned about huge overhead costs: It goes without saying that the businessman does not have to bear the financial burden of paying the rent, phone bills, electricity bills pertaining to the office space or warehouse, or on buying stationery. You only need to think about managing the website and its fixed costs.

4. This type of enterprise involves less risk: You are not under any pressure to sell the products. You do not lose anything if your goods are not sold. If you cannot scale the store or earn profits, you can simply back out. So, the dropshipping model is a less risky form of business.

5. It does not depend on a location: You can carry on your business from anywhere. Therefore, you can be free from the hassles of maintaining an office, employees, and a warehouse. Since the business is independent

of the location and is not tied to some concrete space, you can sit on a beach, or travel to your favorite resort and still make profits.

6. You can sell a varied assortment of products: It is possible to find a dropshipping supplier for nearly everything that you may wish to sell. There are so many options to choose from. You may rely on a single incredible product, sell different goods at the same time, or mix the popular products with the less popular ones. You are the master of your choice. All you have to do is select your niche. You will surely find a supplier for it.

7. You have more resources and time to augment your business: Traditional business models of business require more investment of resources and more work to earn more profits. While in dropshipping you just need to send a larger number of orders to the dropship supplier. The supplier will do the rest for you. But all the profits will be credited to your account.

It takes less time to manage a dropshipping business, and it is almost automated.

Consequently, you have more time on your hands to make plans and boost your business.

8. There will be less damaged goods and less loss: Goods are shipped directly by the suppliers to the buyers. So fewer shipment steps are involved. This greatly decreases the chances of damaging the goods while moving them from place to place.

9. It is convenient for the retailer and the supplier: The retailer does not have to bear the burden of packaging and shipping the products. The supplier does not have the responsibility of promoting and marketing his products. Both of them gain decent profits in the business. So, the dropshipping model is convenient for both of them.

10. Work with multiple suppliers: It is possible for the dropshippers to work with a number of wholesalers at the same time.

11. Easy to scale or remodel: They can be scaled easily both vertically and horizontally. Dropshipping stores are totally digital. They do not need a place to keep the stocks. So, it is

easy to scale them. Moreover, if one product or niche does not sell well, the retailer can conveniently switch over to some items which sell better.

12. No need for spending on an inventory: The retailer does not have to buy a product until he sells it and is paid for it by the customer.

In fact, the retailer has access to an unlimited inventory. If the supplier has an item, the retailer can easily put it up for selling on his website without spending any extra money.

Disadvantages of Dropshopping

But every coin has two sides. The downside of the dropshipping model of business is:

1. The profit margin is slightly lower compared to those of a wholesaler and manufacturer: According to your requirements, location, or niche, the vendors or suppliers may charge higher rates for dropshipping the goods. This impinges on the profit margin to some extent.

2. The liability for the entire transaction rests on the retailer: The customer purchases the item from the website of the retailer. The goods are sold in his name. So even if the supplier makes a mistake, the retailer is held responsible for it. Therefore, it is extremely important to select the right person as your supplier.

3. The retailer has less control over the packaging: Usually, a customer's satisfaction is linked with the personalized branding and packaging of the goods that are shipped. The small details like the notes and freebies that

are given with the order make a lot of difference.

Unfortunately, the retailers do not get a chance to decide the way in which the goods will be presented at the time of delivery. This part of the transaction is mainly dependent on the supplier's choice.

Nevertheless, you can ask your supplier to brand things in a particular way. But you may have to pay some extra money for this service.

4. Some problems may arise because of shipping complications: It is a good idea to sell multiple items to increase sales and thereby boost your profits. But in case, you have a number of suppliers who supply different things this technique may prove to be counter-productive.

Different suppliers charge different rates for shipping according to the location, kind of goods, and some other factors. By chance, if a particular customer orders a number of things which have to be shipped by different suppliers, it will be a difficult task for the retailer. He will be required to calculate and pay the charges for shipping separately to each supplier. If he transfers the various shipping costs to the buyer, it will have a negative impact, and the profit margin may go down.

5. There is a lot of competition: The dropshipping model is very lucrative and popular. So, the number of sellers in every niche and segment is also large. Until a retailer caters to a very specific niche or segment the competition can be detrimental.

6. It can be a tricky affair to manage the inventory: It is almost impossible to keep an account of the supplier's stock. Lack of proper communication or wrong messages could lead to cancellations or delays. Although it is possible to tackle such problems with the help of software, it may increase the overhead costs and prove to be expensive.

Chapter III:
How to Start Up?

Starting an enterprise based on the dropshipping model is an easy way to earn money online. The progress of Shopify, eBay, Amazon, Etsy, and other platforms and marketplaces online has made it possible for anyone to start a store online even for a negligible amount of twenty dollars.

If you are planning to start one dropshipping business like a side occupation or as an alternative to your full-fledged job just follow these simple steps and embark on your dream venture.

Hundreds of people all over the world make 5, 6, and 7 figure incomes by dropshipping their goods. So, you can also do it.

The Steps to be taken to Start a Dropshipping Business

There are five easy steps to launch your dropshipping business. They are:

- Choose a profitable niche for dropshipping
- Find a reliable dropship supplier
- Get an ID for sales tax
- Choose a selling platform
- Implement a strategy for customer acquisition

The things needed for starting a dropshipping enterprise

Apart from genuine motivation, positive attitude, and good work ethics, there are just a few things that are needed for starting this type of business venture.

They are as follows:

- A product for selling
- A person who supplies that item

- A platform where you can sell it

- Sales tax identification

Dropshipping is a digital business. Before embarking on your venture, you must study how feasible it is. You have to think about the following things:

- How will your dropshipping enterprise work?
- Which products are you going to dropship?
- Are there any trending products in your niche?
- In which dropshipping niche there is low competition?
- Dropshipping is suitable for which country?
- Which marketing platform are you going to use for selling your products?

After considering all these points, you can embark on your dropshipping venture.

'Step I: Select the Products

You should select the products for which there is a demand so that you can run your dropshipping store successfully. There are many ways in which you can choose the items.

- You can use Google Trends or Product Mafia to help you in selecting the products.

- You can test which product actually sells online before choosing a product.

You can also choose a sub-niche for selling your items. For instance, yoga pants belong to a very popular sub-niche. You can sell only yoga pants in your store.

Keep these points in mind while selecting the products:

1. The price should be within fifty dollars. So that it is possible for the people to buy them easily online.

2. The option for ePacket delivery should be

enabled for them.

3. They should be ordered in large volumes on AliExpress, Amazon, and eBay. This will confirm that they are actually being bought by people.

4. Google Trends should show upward trends for these products.

Step II: Find a Supplier

It is very important to partner with the right person to supply things. Your business can be ruined if the supplier is not chosen correctly. So, you should not take this step in haste. Choose a supplier after conducting thorough research.

Most of the dropshipping suppliers are stationed overseas so communication plays a vital role. They should be able to understand the orders and respond in a timely manner. Do not select a supplier until you are 100% sure about his communication abilities.

Alibaba is an important online resource which can help you to find and interact with potential suppliers and manufacturers. You should ask them plenty of questions to find out their production capacity and to know how suitable they are for the business.

You can also learn from the experience of other entrepreneurs in the field by reading the business blogs where they discuss dropshipping.

Dropshipping suppliers can be found on shopping

websites like DHGate, DX, AliExpress, and others. You can look for them on portals like DOBA, Wholesale2B, and Worldwide Brands.

Besides AliExpress the other estores from where you may get the goods for selling are:

- DHGate: You can get all the things found on AliExpress over here. Except that the prices are a little higher. For example, if the cost of an item is $9 on the former website, it may be available for $11 here. So, you have to do some research before purchasing things.

- DealExtreme: It does not have a very big inventory but is good for electrical or mechanical products.

- BangGood: It is not a manufacturer's market place but an e-commerce store. So, the goods are more expensive.

- TomTop: It has nearly one lakh items. It is good for tech products.

Step III: Get a Sales Tax License

In order to set up your enterprise, you need to have a tax ID, reseller or retail license, vendor's license, resale certificate, resale number, or sales tax identification.

Actually, sales tax is levied on the sale of products to consumers. It is equal to nearly 6% to 9% of the selling price. Businesses add this amount to the price of the goods and pass on this expense to the consumers.

In order to get this ID, it may be necessary for you to be one business entity, sole proprietor, or a company.

However, this identification may not be absolutely necessary in all places.

Step IV: Choose a Platform for Selling

After you decide which product to sell and find a supplier for it the next step is to choose an online marketplace or selling platform to sell your product and earn money. You can choose to sell on some established marketplace like Amazon, and eBay, or start your own online store.

You can use dropshipping platforms like Shopify or WooCommerce to set up your dropshipping store.

In case, you are absolutely new to the field Shopify can be quite helpful. But it may be a bit costly as you may have to upgrade the package when you wish to scale your store.

While WooCommerce is a WordPress plugin which is free of cost. There are other paid plugins like AliDropship, YouDroop, or WooDropship which can be useful if you do not want to do the work manually.

Choose the Domain Name

Actually, there are two kinds of dropshippers. Some of them have a number of dropshipping stores. They do not pay much attention to their brand name. They use EMDs, exact matching domain names or adopt a sub-niche. They use a name similar to the niche.

The other type of dropshipper has only one store. Their aim is to create a brand. They genuinely work to widen its prospects. They resort to paid marketing for selling their goods online and also make efforts to increase the organic traffic for their website. So first they choose a name very carefully and after that register their domain.

Therefore, while selecting a single domain, or many domains you should consider which kind of dropshipper you are aspiring to be and then go ahead and get them registered.

You can use Namecheap or GoDaddy for getting the domains. They are trustworthy websites. Often, they offer coupons to those who register their domains.

Select the Hosting Platform

You can use Shopify, WooCommerce, or any other dropshipping platform for your business. Shopify is totally automated. In order to set up one basic store using Shopify, you may have to pay $100 per month.

If you choose to use WooCommerce, you will need to pay the domain and hosting charges only. In case, you want to host a number of stores you may host all the domains on one host alone.

Another good option is to use Cloudways to host the e-commerce store. It enables you to set up the store just by clicking a few times. It offers optimized hosting and ensures that the site loads at lightning speed. You only have to pay for those resources which you consumed.

Pick One Dropshipping Plugin

Even if there is enough money at your disposal and you can hire some web design company for creating a customized website initially it is better to use a plugin. Once the site is established and a large amount of revenue starts coming in, you may explore more ways to customize the website.

The process of setting up a store is a bit difficult. So, although you can do dropshipping without a plugin it is better to use it. Plugins enable you to automate the entire process. It is quite easy and convenient to use them.

Some of the plugins which can be used for a WooCommerce store are as follows:

- AliDropship: You can buy this for $86. It can be connected to your store and used for importing the dropship products automatically. You can import goods from AliExpress. After that, you can set the prices on your own. This plugin can be used for only one website. If you launch a new store, you will have to buy another one.

- WooDropship: This freemium plugin integrates easily with WooCommerce. There is an independent repository of goods which can be imported to a dropshipping store just with a click.

Dropfield is a plugin which can be used with both WooCommerce and Shopify. It is like the AliDropship plugin. It allows you to import goods from AliExpress. But you have to pay $47 - $99 per month for it.

You should avoid giving people the idea that you are importing goods from AliExpress. Try to brand your own website as an e-commerce store.

Step V: Create a Plan to Acquire Customers

A great website with an amazing product is of no use for a business if there are no customers. There are a number of ways in which you can catch the attention of customers and draw them to your site.

Starting an ad campaign on Facebook is a very effective option. It gives you a chance to place an offer directly before the targeted audience. It provides you with an opportunity for competing with some of the largest retailers and brands. You can start generating sales and revenues at the beginning. This, in turn, can help to scale the business quickly.

Besides this, you should also focus on email marketing. You can set up automatic email sequences which give discounts and make special offers. This will enable you to leverage the customer base which is already there, and you will not have to spend money on additional marketing and advertising to generate revenue.

Analyze and then optimize

Once your business gets started, you should track all the metrics and the data available to scale your business. You can use Google Analytics and other conversion data to track all the conversions. You should know from where the buyer originated and the path, he took on the website which ultimately led to the sale of a product. In this way, you can enhance the things which worked and eliminate the ones which did not work.

Chapter IV:
What are the Different Ways for Dropshipping? (Amazon FBA, eBay, Shopify, Affiliate Marketing)

After you have chosen a product, partnered with a supplier and set up your business, you have to sell your product. You have to find a way to exhibit your products before the prospective customers. Many alternatives are available for this purpose. You can choose one of them. Or else, you can decide to use Amazon, eBay, and your online store together for selling.

Use Amazon for Dropshipping

It is a very popular online marketplace. It has approximately 300 million users. Over 1 lakh sellers earned more than 1 lakh dollars on Amazon in 2016. It provides additional services like Amazon Prime and Fulfillment facilities.

Amazon is a platform which enables third parties to sell used or new products for fixed prices. The items bought from third parties on Amazon can be fulfilled by using the FBM or FBA options. FBM products are stored in the inventory of the 3rd party. The merchant who is the 3rd party handles the customer service and shipping. FBA products are stocked in the fulfillment centers of Amazon. The customer service and shipping are managed by Amazon.

Third parties can take any one of the three paths on Amazon. They are retail arbitrage, wholesale, and private label.

So even though Amazon stocks many products and sells them, third-party vendors also sell their products through Amazon's website. Actually, Amazon facilitates the sale of goods and helps to sort out things if there are any problems.

Things to Know While Dropshipping Through Amazon

It is important to work in accordance with the policy for dropshippers on Amazon.

- You should write your contact details and not that of the supplier on every sale.

- You are responsible for the returns.

- You have to utilize the services of an independent supplier and not another merchant of Amazon.

The Advantages of Using Amazon for Selling

- Selling items on Amazon have similar advantages like eBay. It is easy to start your business, you can access a huge audience instantly, and there is no need to be concerned about SEO or marketing.

- Amazon has fulfillment warehouses which enables you to dropship your items without bearing the burden of warehousing, packing, or shipping.

The Disadvantages of Using Amazon for Selling

- Listing fees: In order to access this wide network of customers you have to pay a substantial amount as commission fees. The charges are based on the type of goods and are usually between the range of ten percent to fifteen percent. So, if you work with small profit margins of dropshipping, this can take away a big chunk from your profits.

- Sales data is exposed: When you use Amazon's platform, all the sales data can be seen by Amazon. It knows what items you sell best and how much you sell. So, it can use this information for identifying the good opportunities for selling and increase its involvement in that niche and eventually push out the other vendors who sell through its platform.

- No long-lasting relationship with the buyers: Just like eBay you may not have a long-term connection with the buyers. The website aims to help itself. So, it focuses on the goods and not on the merchants. There are restrictions on the way you brand your enterprise, display your goods, and interact with the buyers.

- No customization: There is no scope for customization. Everything from branding to marketing is under the control of Amazon.

Use eBay for Dropshipping

This site is well known as it is the world's biggest auction website for physical products online. Here are a few reasons why you can choose to use eBay or avoid using it for dropshipping.

It has approximately 171 million users, and nearly 1 billion goods are listed in 190 markets. It provides an option for auction and operates as a standard retail platform online.

The Advantages of Using eBay for Selling

1. It is easy to start working: You can join eBay by creating an account. Soon after that, you can add a list of your wholesale goods. That's all that you have to do to start your business.

2. You can access a big audience: Many online customers visit eBay which is an auction giant. So, when you put up a list of your goods on eBay millions of buyers will see the listings. Such an active and robust market will ensure that you can sell your items at a good price.

3. Less marketing: Since you are supported by an enormous platform, there is no need to bother about SEO, marketing, or paying money for traffic. It helps to save your time because marketing is a big challenge associated with the launching of a dropshipping enterprise.

The Disadvantages of Using eBay for Selling

1. Fees for listing: The biggest drawback of using eBay for selling is that you are required to pay some fees. The most important one is a success fee. It can be equal to ten percent or more of the selling price of your products. The profit margins in dropshipping are already quite low. This fee can reduce your profits further.

2. Re-listing and constant monitoring: It uses the auction method. Hence, you have to monitor the work constantly and re-list the goods you wish to sell. Although, there are some tools for automating this process it is not as simple as listing some static item on one's own website and selling it.

3. You cannot customize the sales platform: You

have to follow the eBay templates for listing your products. So, it is not possible to create some professional page for adding value to your items.

4. **Not possible to have a connection with the customers for a long-term:** You may have some repeat eBay buyers, but most of the customers may not buy things from you a second time. Even if you gain some goodwill through your excellent service, it may not last long.

   The structure of the marketplace is meant to be useful for itself. It wants to give importance to the products and not to the merchants. There will be restrictions regarding your communication with the customers, the way of branding, and designing your store.

5. **You do not create an asset:** If you have a store which has repeat buyers and generates traffic you build a business that is an asset and can be sold to someone. When you use eBay for selling, you do not build a long-lasting brand. Your business does not have tangible value and cannot be sold.

Use Etsy for Dropshipping

It has approximately 54 million people as members, nearly 2 million sellers, and around 32 million buyers. It is popularly used by women, and 84% of the sellers are women. It is a trendy marketplace which focuses on arts, handmade goods, and crafts.

The main advantage of using these platforms is that the customers trust these marketplaces. While chief disadvantages are that firstly, you have to compete directly with the other retailers on the platform. Secondly, customers have a lot of choice in one place.

Use Shopify for Dropshipping

Shopify is an e-commerce firm which has its headquarters in Ottawa. It offers a set of services to online retailers to make things easier for running their online stores. They include marketing, shipping, payment services, and tools to engage customers.

Nearly 6 lakh merchants use its platform, and its gross merchandise exceeds $82 billion.

You can find items for selling on Shopify using Oberlo. It helps to find and also add items directly to your own Shopify store which you can sell right away.

- Oberlo is an expert in dropshipping. It can keep the items for you so that you do not have to maintain a warehouse. When you get an order for some product you can just send the details to Oberlo. It will take care of the packaging and shipping of the item. It has a supplier network for this purpose.

- Hundreds of thriving Shopify merchants use Oberlo to run their online stores. It gives you a chance to concentrate on building the business and marketing as you do not have to waste time on packing and shipping the orders.

- Oberlo grows with your enterprise. When you build your team or hire staff, you can add more accounts. You can expand your catalog of products. For example, if you sell shoes, you can start selling socks, too.

- You can build a relationship with suppliers. Using Oberlo, you can communicate with the suppliers and ensure that your customers get the best possible experience.

Use Your Online Store
for Dropshipping

Instead of selling via third-party websites like eBay and Amazon you can establish your own store for selling products online. This option is very attractive for those who want to set up a flourishing dropshipping business.

The Advantages of Using Your Online Store for Selling

- More control: If you have your own store you can create such an environment for shopping that is conducive for selling your goods and gives more value to the customers. It is possible for you to customize the appearance and layout of the website. You can create customized product pages which are optimized to inform your clients about the goods.

- It can be designed easily: It is easy to build an e-commerce store with the help of Shopify. You just have to choose one store design from hundreds of choices that are available. Then make the customizations according to your preferences, add the products, and finalize a payment method. That's all that you have to do to set up your store. It can be ready in a day's time.

- Mobile ready: It can be a difficult task to sell on eBay or Amazon through a mobile. While your own online store will be more responsive if it is built properly. That means it is going to look amazing on a mobile phone or an iPad. This is important because nowadays around thirty percent of online buying is done through some mobile device.

Shopify allows you to manage the entire business using a mobile device. It is very useful for the owners of dropshipping businesses because they often run the business while they are going from one place to another.

- No need to pay fees to a third-party: There is no need to pay ten percent to fifteen percent of the sale to a third-party like Amazon or eBay.

So, your profit will increase significantly.

- You build a long-lasting business: You can build a business which lasts long, has acknowledged expertise, a distinctive touch, and repeat buyers. Most importantly, you will build an enterprise with equity. It is much easier to sell one business which is built around a website that is owned independently.

- The absence of direct competition: You are not required to compete directly with other sellers who sell the same product on a common platform.

The Disadvantages of Using Your Online Store for Selling

- You get less traffic: If you have your own website you have to bear the responsibility of getting traffic paid advertising, SEO, and marketing.

- You have to pay for web hosting.

- It takes some time to get a ranking on Google.

Use Affiliate Marketing
for Dropshipping

This form of marketing is performance-based. An affiliate is rewarded for each customer or visitor he brings to the company's website through his marketing efforts.

This type of marketing uses common methods available on the Internet for marketing like paid SEM, organic SEO, PPC, email marketing, display marketing, and content marketing. Affiliates also utilize less orthodox methods like publishing reviews for their partner's goods and services.

Affiliate marketing and referral marketing both utilize third parties for driving traffic to the company. But they are different in the sense that the former relies on financial motivation while the latter banks on personal relationships and trust.

In this type of marketing, a person has to partner with some e-commerce store or join some affiliate program. He sells the goods of a particular company for which he does the marketing. In return, he gets a fixed commission. The company decides the amount of commission to be given. It is paid on the basis of how many goods are sold through the person's reference.

Affiliate programs for dropshipping are increasing day by day because more people have started using the profitable dropshipping business model.

Some Affiliate Programs for Dropshipping

- AliDropship: You can get an affiliate commission of $284 for each sale.

- Salehoo: The commission is equal to 50% for each sale.

- WooDropship: It offers 30% commissions.

- Volusion: You can choose between a referral commission plan or a reseller discount as an affiliate commission.

- Dropified: Earn 30% of the buyer's monthly subscription fees.

Chapter V:
Market Research and How to Find a Niche

Comprehensive market research will enable you to establish your business on a strong foundation. In order to gain an insight into the market, you need to perform keyword research, understand the impact of seasonality, and observe your competitors. You should consider factors like age range, gender, and demographics.

While choosing a suitable product to sell, see if its retail price, size and weight, durability, and turnover rate are suitable. Also, think about the items for which cross-selling tactics can be used.

Know Your Niche and Target Market Better

Lao Tzu has rightly said, "The journey of a thousand miles starts with a single step."

Follow these steps to find out more about your niche and target market. Your hard work and commitment will surely be rewarded.

Step 1: Keyword Research

First of all, you should assess the present demand for the product you are planning to sell. You can use KWFinder to determine the ranking of the chosen product's keyword monthwise. This will help you to know the number of people who use search engines such as Google to search for a particular product every month. Thus, you will have a rough idea of the demand for the product.

Ideally, if you aspire to build a business on the basis of some product, its keyword should appear thousands of times in the monthly searches. However, if the product is for some new market which is just coming up then many people would not have searched for it.

Step 2: Understand the Impact of Seasonality

Secondly, you should make an effort to comprehend the way in which seasonality could influence the customer's buying patterns. There are particular products which are merely seasonal items and their demand changes on the basis of seasonal factors while others do well all around the year.

Guesswork is not sufficient for finding out about these two types of commodities. You can utilize Google Trends for this purpose. It gives a graphical view of the seasons in which a particular product was demanded the most.

Forecasts about the trends can enable you to be well prepared for the high and low levels of sale all through the year.

Step 3: Identify and Observe Your Competitors

Finally, you should recognize the competition and comprehend the way in which your business rivals carry on their transactions. Search for their websites and see their presence in social platforms and marketplaces like eBay, and Amazon. Look at their ratings and reviews carefully. See what the customers say about them. Observe keenly and find out if there is anything in which they are lacking and are unable to meet the expectations of the market. So that you can use that opportunity to fill up the gap.

Factors to be Kept in Mind while Analyzing the Target Market

Age Range

Understanding the spending and buying patterns of various age groups is very useful. It is a known fact that the young adults who were born in between the years 1980 to 2000 belong to a low-income bracket. Statistics show that they spend less. So dropshipping costly products which specifically target this age range is not advisable. Similarly, those who belong to the sixty plus age group do not find it very convenient to buy things which are dropshipped or sold online.

Demographics

A knowledge of the geographic or physical location and the income bracket of the target audience is essential. It will enable you to know the size of your audience, and where the majority of the audience is available, and the way in which you can offer the dropshipped goods to them.

Kind of Institution

Will you be selling the items directly to the customers, other enterprises, or the government organizations? Several aspects of the business are influenced by your choice to sell the dropshipped products B2C that is business to the consumers, B2B means business to another business or B2G which implies business to the government. It determines who your clients are, the numbert of goods they buy, their chief goal for buying your products, the way in which you provide your goods to them.

Generally, you sell directly to the consumers while dropshipping. Consider the way in which it will influence your business as a whole.

Gender

Statistics show that women and men shop differently. Their spending and buying patterns differ in the context of general products as well as in the case of dropshipped goods. Though it is not so important to know the potential target market's gender, it can prove to be helpful.

The type of devices they utilize for shopping, the type of content that matters for them, for instance, product descriptions and testimonials, the sort of language which could trigger customer conversion, are some factors which can be influenced by the gender.

Know the Level of Competition

It is necessary to know about the competition that exists in the market for a particular product so that you can deal with it. If already there are established sellers for the item which you wish to sell it is a positive sign. But if the number of sellers for the same item is very big, it may be difficult for your enterprise to gain importance.

To find out the level of competition, you can utilize these tactics:

Use Tools Available Online

There are site explorers like SEMrush which help you in checking the domain authority and rank of a website using a URL. You can use them to get a clear picture of the amount of traffic that is driven to their website from keywords as well as from other links. You can also personally observe their sites and get an insight into the way they function.

Order Items from Your Competitors

There may be a difference between what appears online and the real things that take place. So, it is a good idea to order something from your competitor's website. This will enable you to become familiar with the peculiarities that make them a unique enterprise, or the negative aspects of the brand experience provided by them. You may even get some tips to improve your own enterprise.

However, there is no need to copy their entire process of working. Just observe if there are any flaws which you can avoid and improve your customer's experience.

Analyze Your Competitor's Social Network

The social channels of your competitor are an important means of getting direct feedback from the customers about his business. They also provide a basis on which you can analyze your rival's marketing strategy. You can check how well their brand is performing and what are the flaws. You can work on these to enhance your brand.

Find the Right Items
for Dropshipping

First of all, search on Google for the potential item you would like to sell. You will see the autocomplete options which are actually the most used keywords that your potential suppliers or customers are searching for. If you want, you can look further into the autocomplete results. This will help you to give proper direction to your brand strategy because you will be able to find terms which are related to it.

Besides this, Google search will also show "related searches." They are basically similar keywords which are very frequently used search phrases.

Checking the review sites and product forums are one more way of choosing your product on the basis of consumer demand. First, see the comments and get to know what the kinds of products people want and after that supply them.

You can also find out which products are popular by looking at their ranking in review sites. If you sell goods which have a higher rank, there are more chances of selling a larger number of goods.

Some products which have been very popular for some time are:

- Phone accessories

- Jewelry

- Custom-made T-shirts

- Custom-made phone cases

- Custom-made mugs

- Healthy foods

- Baby products

- Skincare products

- Camping gear

- Fitness and gym equipment

The Way to Find the Best Products for Dropshipping

To be successful in any e-commerce endeavor, it is very important to find out the best products for selling. But for dropshipping this task holds the most vital position.

Though there is no foolproof way to find the product which is absolutely right for dropshipping you can make a decision on the basis of some available facts and figures, and by doing research on what items can be sold.

Hyacil Han, the author of 'Dropshipping Ultimate Guide: The Expeditive and Accessible Scheme to Earn a Substantial Revenue at Home' has advised, "Don't find customers for your products, find products for your customers."

The criteria for choosing the best products for dropshipping is as follows:

Retail Price

The wholesale and retail price play a crucial role in dropshipping. If the prices are low more people will buy things, but you will earn less profit per item. In case, the prices are high people will purchase fewer items, but you will gain a higher profit on each item.

So, you have to strike a balance between your profit margins and the expectations of the customers. In dropshipping as a retailer, you should aim for 15% to 45% profit margins. This implies that it is optimal to price the products between $50 - $100.

Size and Weight

The packaging, as well as the shipping costs for different products, are based on the packaging material needed and the manual or other effort involved in shipping them. So, it is cheaper to dropship small and light items. They offer the biggest profit margins. It may be possible to drop ship larger products also with relatively large margins, but it is always preferable to start with the small items.

Cross-Selling Items

Selling a set of related items together enables you to provide more value and encourage your customers to buy more things each time they place an order. Think about the things which serve a similar purpose and can be sold together. For instance, if you are dropshipping easels, you can also drop ship paint brushes, canvases, and other items related to art work.

If you adopt this method think of a way to price the products in a strategic manner so that the sale is beneficial for you and your customer as well. You may decide to sell the main item for a low-profit-margin like 10% or 15%, in order to encourage the customer to purchase it. Then cross-sell the other components and accessories at a higher rate like 100% and make up the lost profit.

Durability

If you sell disposable or renewable products, there are more chances of getting orders repeatedly. This can enhance your sales. Often retailers offer subscription options to their customers. It ensures that they repeat the purchases. If you want to make it more attractive, you can provide a discount to the people who subscribe to the service.

Turnover rate

This refers to the rate of changes in the product. As the retailer of a particular online store, you will have to put up photographs of the product and publish content about it to promote your business. All this requires time and expenditure.

If the product you sell undergoes change, is updated or discounted within short time spans you will be required to change the content often and thereby spend more money on it.

Seek Substantial Profits

In the dropshipping model of business, you have to focus on marketing. You have to make efforts to acquire customers. So, the hard work that you do for selling a $20 product is basically equal to the work that you do for selling a product that is worth $1,500.

Therefore, you should choose a niche where you can gain more profits.

Shipping Costs Should Be Low

Try to find such products which do not have very high shipping costs. Even though the manufacturer or supplier handles the shipping, high costs can repel the customers. Moreover, if the shipping costs are low, you can offer free shipping and attract more customers and thereby increase your sales. While the small number of shipping costs can easily be absorbed in the business expenses.

See to it that Your Product is Appealing for Impulse Buyers who have a Disposable Income

Your goal is to drive the maximum traffic to the website, and you want the highest possible conversion rate so that your business can flourish. Therefore, you should sell such products which encourage impulsive buying and are appealing for those who have the financial capacity to purchase things at once.

Ensure that the People are Looking for the Product

Check some search terms which are commonly used while looking for your niche. For this, you can use tools like the Keyword Planner or Trends offered by Google. If nobody has searched for the item that you are thinking of selling, then you should give up the idea of selling it as you will not make any sales.

Look for a Product which You Can Brand as Your Own

Dropshipping can be more impressive if it is possible for you to rebrand things that you sell and show as if they belong to your own brand. So, you should try to find items on which you can put your own labels and sell with customized branding and packaging.

Sell Things which are Not Easily Available Locally

If you choose to sell something which is not readily available in the local areas it may be more attractive for potential customers.

Mistakes to Be Avoided while Selecting a Product

1. Do not choose a product on the basis of what you like or dislike. Make it a point to decide on the basis of facts and research. Carefully evaluate its demand in the market.

2. Avoid selling "true copies." It is a cheap trick and will not have a good impression on the customers. Besides this, it is illegal to do so.

3. Do not sell a product just because others are selling it. Usually, the market which caters to the trending items is very saturated. Therefore, there is a high level of competition. In case, you wish to sell such products conduct thorough research and become familiar with the rising and falling trends so that you know the expectations of your customers.

Chapter VI:
Tips for Succeeding with Your Online Business

Mostly dropshipping products are sold on the basis of impulse buying. So there is a need to push the items right under the nose of the prospective buyers instead of just waiting for them to visit the dropshipping store.

Dropshipping goods are promoted by means of search engines, marketing platforms, and social media which charge some remuneration for the service. Even a personal network can be used for this purpose.

Promoting the Products on Social Platforms

Social media is one amongst the most powerful means to promote, distribute content, advertise, and to acquire customers. For example, Facebook has more than one and a half billion users with varied backgrounds and lifestyles. So naturally, it is a very attractive platform for digital marketers to promote their products.

You can use these platforms for popularizing your product. But you should remember that content plays a vital role. Even if the platform is big and the product is great if it does not have an impressive content to back it, your efforts will be futile.

It has been tested and confirmed that people purchase dropshipping products from platforms like Facebook, Pinterest, and Instagram.

Influencer Marketing on Instagram

Nowadays, influencer marketing occupies an important place in the customer acquisition plans of online retailers. It is especially very effective for trendy niches. For example, if you want to sell a new type of handbag and you ask a popular figure on Instagram to include your handbag in one of her posts and tag your business, you are sure to win a big batch of new customers.

You can use Instagram influencers to promote your products. These are the people who have a large following on Instagram. They are of three types: celebrities, social influencers, and micro influencers.

- Celebrities: Movie actors, sportspersons, artists, politicians, and social workers belong to this category. They are powerful and generally do not work with small enterprises.

- Social influencers: They have more than ten thousand followers. They do not restrict themselves to one niche alone. They charge high rates for promotion work and usually work with more than one brand at a time.

- Micro influencers: They have five thousand to ten thousand followers. They are confined to a niche. They can be very helpful for promoting the products which belong to only one niche. They charge lower rates for promoting your posts.

If you choose to do influencer marketing pick one niche and select influencers who are more impressive, make sure that their post has a minimum of five hearts or comments.

Start pitching after you have noted down the names of 5 - 10 influencers. You can tell them that they may keep the item if they post its picture in their account on Instagram.

Google Ads and Facebook Ads

Google and Facebook advertising are different in nature. Google shows advertisements which are related to the keywords used for searching by the user. While Facebook Ads function on the basis of user information. The interests of the users are noted which are called data points. It displays ads on the basis of these data points for the users.

Benefits of Google Ads

- You can gain good exposure in the search results.

- They give you a chance to advertise on the world's largest platforms like YouTube, and Google search.

- It is easy to target specific demographics like language, location, and device.

- You can use high volume key phrases or keywords which are related to the niche you are dealing with and maximize exposure.

Benefits of Facebook Ads

- They help you to start your business easily.

- You can control the amount of money you spend every day.

- It is possible for you to target specific demographics like location, and interests.

- You can get quick results.

- They are useful for increasing brand awareness.

- Good ads or boosted posts can become viral.

PPC Advertising

PPC advertising is allowed on many social media platforms. Facebook ads are an example of this. Another platform which is popular for advertising is Google AdWords.

Customer Reviews and Ratings

Customer reviews make a lot of difference in this type of enterprise. Just a few negative reviews can actually ruin the entire business. You can see how people buy products online from eBay and Amazon. The decision to purchase things on the basis of the rating of the product and the comments of the customers about it.

The same thing is applicable to your dropshipping store. A few good reviews can boost the reputation of your website and products. The best way of getting accolades from the customers is to cater to them in the best possible manner.

If you offer high-quality goods, a remarkable customer support service and quick delivery of items, you can surely make your mark and get good feedback from the customers.

This feedback can be utilized as a testimonial for the website and can help to acquire more customers.

Email Marketing

You can use email marketing to inform your clients about the changes in your company. You can inform them about the price changes, and the discounts offered. Emails may be used for conveying content related to the product or the industry.

MailChimp can be very useful for this purpose. It automates some processes, creates and saves templates, and produces analytics and reports.

This type of marketing is more complex and is usually used for the purpose of remarketing. That means after collecting your buyers' emails, you can sell your new products to them by sending the information about the products through email. You can use automation software such as Campaign Monitor, GetResponse, MailChimp, or AWeber for this purpose.

Customer Support

An efficient customer support service can provide better customer satisfaction and thereby help to boost your business.

You can adopt any of these methods which are generally used by the e-commerce industry. They are:

- Phone support: Phone is a quick and efficient means of connecting with the client directly. It is easier to deal with tricky situations by phone. It also enables you to get quick feedback from your client. Google Voice can be useful for this purpose.

- Email support: You can use email for providing support to your customers. It is a good idea to create emails which bear the name of your domain, for example, hello@domainname.com. This will give it a professional look, and your brand will be impressive for the customers. You can use Helpscout which is a very suitable software for email support.

- Support through social media: Sometimes customers look at the pages of the brands on social media even before they contact a particular brand. The customers can find answers to their questions there as social media which is a forum for the public already has answers for them.

A good representative who provides customer support through social media can help to set up good relations between the brand and the customers.

- Live chat: Many brands incorporate the live chatting facility on the websites to provide customer support. This method has become very popular. It enables customers to get support quickly. It is less intimidating than posting questions on some public forum.

But if your business has not expanded much this type of support is not needed. This option may be suitable after you have scaled your business. Another option is to utilize the facility for direct messages on Twitter and Instagram or use   Facebook Messenger.

Other Marketing Methods

There are some marketing strategies which are inexpensive or free of cost but have slow results. Some of them are:

Forum or Blog Marketing

You can look for forums or blogs which are associated with your niche or products and actively participate in the discussions. You can represent your particular niche and include your website's link. In this way, you may increase the traffic and get new customers to your online store.

Growth Hacking

This method is not expensive, and at the same time, it is highly effective to get creative campaigns for marketing online. Retargeting the old campaigns or appearing as guest bloggers for popular websites in your niches are some examples of growth hacking. Essentially it comprises of content marketing.

Content Marketing

This involves a process of creating valuable content to acquire an audience which can be converted into customers. It is not an explicit way of advertising. The content should be about serving the audience than about serving your brand. It can be in the form of a trendy Instagram post, a witty post on Twitter, or a blog.

Conclusion

You should keep trying out new products and harmonize your campaigns with the growing trends. The advantage of the dropshipping model is that it is possible to learn by testing one's ideas and products. If there is something which does not sell, you can just remove it without incurring a loss.

The absence of upfront costs and minimum risks make dropshipping business an exciting venture which can become a flourishing business with a little hard work and commitment.

Hyacil Han has rightly said, "The most successful

people started from NOTHING ... they didn't wait for the opportunity to knock but created the opportunity on their own ... worked hard and made history."

This model of business is very conducive for the retailer because there is no need for a physical location like an office to work or a warehouse to store things. All you require is a connection to the internet and a laptop!

However, it is also very beneficial for the entrepreneurs who have their own offices and warehouses to adopt the dropshipping method for some products. This enables them to free up space and resources for other goods.

Bibliography

1. Shopify. The ultimate guide to Dropshipping. Chapter 2. The supply chain and

fulfillment process. Retrieved from

https://www.shopify.in/guides/dropshipping/supply-chain-and-fulfillment-process

2. Shopify. The ultimate guide to Dropshipping. Chapter 6. Evaluating sales channels.

Retrieved from
https://www.shopify.in/guides/dropshipping/evaluating-sales-channels

3. Richard Lazazzera. A Better Lemonade Stand. Drop Shipping 101: The definitive

guide to building a drop shipping business in 2019 (2018 updated). Retrieved from

https://www.abetterlemonadestand.com/what-is-drop-shipping/

4. Jonathan Long. Founder, Uber Brands. 6 steps to building a successful   online drop

shipping business (2017). Retrieved from

https://www.entrepreneur.com/article/297744

5. Sajjad Shahid. What is dropshipping? How to start it in 2019? (detailed guide)

(updated 2018). Retrieved from

https://www.cloudways.com/blog/what-is-dropshipping/

6. Simon Slade. Salehoo.com. How to start a dropshipping business in 5 easy steps.

Retrieved from

https://www.salehoo.com/blog/how-to-start-a-drop-shipping-business-in-5-easy-steps

7. Bill. High paying affiliate programs. Dropshipping affiliate programs. Retrieved from

https://highpayingaffiliateprograms.com/dropshipping-affiliate-programs/

8. Shopify. Find products to sell online with Oberlo. Retrieved from

https://www.shopify.in/oberlo